A Choice

Shepherd Hoodwin

Summerjoy Press
LAGUNA NIGUEL, CALIFORNIA

ALL IS CHOICE

Summerjoy Press
99 Pearl
Laguna Niguel CA 92677-4818

shoodwin@gmail.com
https://shepherdhoodwin.com

Copyright © 2021 by Shepherd Hoodwin

All rights reserved. No part of this publication may be reproduced, stored in a retrieval system, or transmitted, in any form or by any means, electronic, mechanical, photocopying, recording, or otherwise, without the prior written permission of the publisher, except by a reviewer, who may quote brief passages in a review.

ISBN: 9798586432049

Photograph of Shepherd Hoodwin by John Kilis.

DEDICATION

For

Sarah Chambers

*The first Michael channel,
who began it all*

CONTENTS

DEDICATION — iii
PREFACE — vi

GENERAL PRINCIPLES — 1
  1 • WHY IS CHOICE SO IMPORTANT? — 2
  2 • THE LIMITS OF REALITY CREATION — 12
  3 • OBSERVING OUR THOUGHTS — 14
  4 • REASON — 16
  5 • SELF-VALIDATION — 21
  6 • PREDICTIONS — 22
  7 • THE ROLE OF FEELING — 24
  8 • PRIORITIES — 26
  9 • CONSCIOUSLY CHOOSING — 28
  10 • BLAMING THE VICTIMS — 30
  11 • THE KARMIC WHEEL — 32
  12 • IT'S ALL GOOD — 34

WHAT WE HAVE THE RIGHT TO CHOOSE — 37
  13 • INCARNATIONAL CHOICE — 38
  14 • GOVERNMENT — 39
  15 • RELIGION — 43
  16 • GUIDES — 48

17 • CHOOSING OUR WORDS 51

WHAT WE DON'T HAVE THE RIGHT TO CHOOSE 53
   18 • OTHERS' RIGHT TO CHOOSE 54
   19 • CHILDREN 56
   20 • HIERACHIES 59

   CONCLUSION 60

   ABOUT THE AUTHOR 61
   OTHER BOOKS BY SHEPHERD HOODWIN 63
   REVIEWS 69

PREFACE

The Michael teachings are a fascinating body of spiritual knowledge about how we set up our lifetimes. Michael is a group of souls working cooperatively who have completed their lifetimes on the physical plane. If you're new to the teachings, my site (https://shepherdhoodwin.com) has a glossary, bibliography, and other information, although I have also included definitions in the text.

The word "choice" appears eighty times in the first Michael book, *Messages from Michael* by Chelsea Quinn Yarbro, and one hundred seventy-five times in *More Messages from Michael*. Members of the group of students portrayed in the Yarbro books sometimes lamented hearing yet another lecture about choice from Michael. I've been a Michael channel and student since 1986, yet only recently have I begun to grasp how profound, multi-faceted, and far-reaching the concept that "All is choice" really is.

I hope that this short book will empower you to make choices more consciously and help you to create a life permeated with love, truth, and beauty.

> Shepherd Hoodwin
> Laguna Niguel, California
> January 15, 2021

Part I

GENERAL PRINCIPLES

1 • WHY IS CHOICE SO IMPORTANT?

According to the Michael teachings, we are, at our core, an eternal *spark of the Tao* (or Source). We decided to have an adventure on Earth, and created a new *essence* as our vehicle. We began our journey as humans on the physical plane. Once we are complete with that phase, we will gradually ascend through the higher six planes, activating more layers of our essence, until we're back home full time in the Tao. This loop from the Tao and back again is a *grand cycle.*

The lower part of our essence is our *soul*, which collects our physical plane experiences. It created our current and past-life personalities, and will create those in any future lifetimes. In our first lifetime, our soul is totally inexperienced. Gradually, it moves from being wholly a creation to being a co-creator with our spark, partly through learning how to make choices, which generate experiences. We see the results of our choices and can make adjustments, becoming more skillful as we go along.

It is similar to how creativity works in the arts. For example, composers try a series of chords, listen to them, and perhaps try something different until the result is as pleasing as they can make it. Perhaps they study with teachers who suggest things they hadn't thought of, and that expands their range of creativity.

Will Rogers, the great American humorist, said, "Good judgment comes from experience, and a lot of that comes from bad judgment." In other words, we all make a lot of mistakes on the way to learning how to navigate life more skillfully. Even the greatest composers try a lot of wrong notes before finding those that work. Most of their mature works are more skillful and substantial than their early ones. Prodigies such as Mozart were quite accomplished at an early age; the likeliest explanation is that they developed a lot of their skill in past lives. But even with Mozart, his late works were more profound. If we don't get to make our own choices and therefore our own mistakes, we cannot develop mastery.

Another analogy: The Tao is like parents who have children (essences) that they plan to take into the family business. As newborns, they must be cared for, but as they grow, they learn the business until they can help run it. If the children never take any responsibility and make decisions, they don't learn. Some are fond of saying that we are children of God, but would any parent want its offspring to stay children forever?

Prior to each lifetime, the soul creates a personality made up of *overleaves*, which are traits designed to give the soul the specific kinds of experiences it wants to have in that lifetime. The body, parental imprinting, astrology, and other factors also shape the personality. As a newborn baby, our personality, like the new soul, was totally without experience, although to some degree, we always draw upon the experience of our soul and spark—they can be seen in the background. As we mature and have experiences, our personality increasingly becomes a co-creator with them—like the soul, it becomes more skillful in making choices.

In the Genesis creation story, it says that God formed humans from dust and breathed life into it.

That is how all creation works. We start with raw material. For a painter, that might be a blank canvas and paints. For a writer, that might be a new word processing document. They are inert until we breathe life into them. When we create something that lives, the creation goes on to become a creator. A work of art has a life of its own apart from the artist, perhaps provoking thought or inspiring reflection. It has its own relationship with those who interact with it. It has an energy. I knew of a blind man who used to go to art museums, stand in front of paintings, and feel their energy. He raved to a friend of mine how she had to see the Van Gogh exhibit at the Met!

Every creation expands the creator. The Tao expands by creating universes (and essences within them) that then go on to become co-creators. Essences expand through the soul's creation of personalities. Even after the body that first housed the personality dies, it continues to have experiences and grow on the astral plane (where we go between lifetimes), co-creating with essence until it is fully integrated into it and goes dormant as a sort of subpersonality of essence that enriches it.

We are large, multifaceted beings. Different parts of us are responsible for different kinds of choices. Our spark chose our essence traits, our soul sets up our lifetimes, and our personality has primary responsibility for the specifics of our lifetime, being on the "front lines." The personality itself is multi-faceted, and different parts of it handle different kinds of choices. Ideally, however, personality works in harmony with essence to make the best possible choices. Essence is already in unity with our core, or

1 • WHY IS CHOICE SO IMPORTANT?

spark, so that results in wholeness. When we are in our true identity as our whole self, we understand that "I" made all these choices. We take responsibility for all of them, even if we do not yet fully understand them or have mastery of them.

Many people identify as being their body, or an ego in a bag of skin, as Alan Watts put it. They are cut off from their essence, which is frustrating for both essence and personality. However, every situation brings experiences and therefore can eventually be used for growth. When there are breakthroughs, when personality opens to essence, it can be thrilling, and essence will have learned about going from being imprisoned in an unresponsive personality to freedom. Ultimately, no experience need be wasted.

We are constantly making choices. We choose actions, words, attitudes, etc., both on conscious and unconscious levels. Unconscious choices can come from our own storehouse of thoughts and feelings, many of which we may not yet have brought to the light of awareness, examined, and processed.

They can also come from our hardwired physical instincts, most particularly our survival urge. These are built into our bodies and are designed to operate dumbly so that we don't have to think. For example, fear usually automatically stops us before we accidentally waltz off a cliff. But the survival instinct is a blunt tool that would often push us into inappropriate behavior. Part of the survival instinct is the desire to reproduce—our body may tell us that if we don't have sex now, the whole human race will die out and it will be our fault! This can lead to impulsive behavior and perhaps violations of others.

ALL IS CHOICE

There's nothing wrong with our animal instincts, but they need to come under our control if we wish to live from higher consciousness.

It's amazing how many of our thoughts and feelings don't originate with us personally. We can absorb them from other people without realizing it, especially if we have unresolved issues that resonate with them. These people need not be in our physical presence or even currently in our life to influence us. We are all connected, often in unseen ways.

Some unconscious influences come from our family and cultural imprinting, things we might realize that don't agree with if we take them out and look at them.

Others come from the collective unconscious, a term in Jungian psychology defined as "the part of the unconscious mind which is derived from ancestral memory and experience and is common to all humankind, as distinct from the individual's unconscious." That is the realm of archetypes that speak to us all.

These many forces in our lives often conflict. What determines which one governs any given unconscious choice? There's a certain amount of chaos involved, but one influence is our astrology. If we're living on automatic pilot, an astrological reading might be able to predict our behavior at a given time. Good astrologers, however, teach that we do, in fact, have control over our destiny—astrological influences are like our energetic climate but need not govern our choices.

Overleaves, personality traits defined in the Michael teachings, can also influence automatic choices. In their *positive* (love-based) *poles*, they are used more consciously. In their *negative* (fear-based) *poles,* our *false personality* uses them without consciousness. For example, in *aggression mode*, one is dynamic in the positive pole, but belligerent in the negative—on autopilot, someone in aggression mode may fly off the handle, perhaps regretting it later. When Michael teaches about the obsolescence of the overleaves, they don't mean that we no longer have them. They are normally good tools for what we want to accomplish in a given lifetime. Michael means that we no longer are controlled by them, but instead choose consciously, using the best tools for the situation.

Karma can be a major influence. It is a strong, compelling force, but one can still consciously choose how to deal with it, like skillfully riding a wild horse. Strongly negative karmic debts can be repaid in positive ways. For example, if someone killed you in a past life, you can give them an opportunity to help you in a positive way to repay that debt, such as saving your life literally or figuratively. However, on autopilot, the karma might impel you to kill them.

As we evolve, more of our choices become conscious, and we access a broader palette of possibilities. We make our choices more artistically, bringing more beauty into the world.

Some choices are more significant than others, but seemingly small choices can have a large impact. Every choice is important as practice for creating.

For example, some people have found that keeping a record of all the money they spend and reviewing it regularly, even for a short time, have made them more conscious of their financial choices. Maybe they were surprised by some of them and decided to make changes. Perhaps they created a budget, but simply becoming more conscious of our spending might be enough to bring our finances into better balance.

All humans are evolving simply due to the fact that we're having experiences. When we choose with awareness, engaging with our full faculties, including reason, we make better choices, with more pleasant outcomes, and grow relatively quickly through joy. When we choose on autopilot, we grow relatively slowly, through pain. Either way, the evolution of consciousness is a very long, complex process. If it were quick and simple, we'd only need one lifetime!

(People generally take 100–200 lifetimes to complete the physical plane, depending on their average lifespan, speed of moving through the thirty-five soul age levels, and personal preference. The fewest I know of is 37, and a "specialist in infant mortality" I channeled for has had 1500 lives.)

Good choices could be defined as those that bring positive results and that we still feel good about later. We ourselves are the final arbiter of whether a particular choice we made was the best possible one, and sometimes that is not clear until much later. However, being mindful during the process of making choices tends to bring better results.

Reviewing past choices as honestly and objectively as possible can help us to make better ones. Considering the deeper reasons we made poor

1 • WHY IS CHOICE SO IMPORTANT?

ones and working on those issues can be a powerful tool for growth. Reviewing the reasons we made positive choices when we normally wouldn't have can also be growthful, reinforcing those behaviors.

What looks like a good choice to one person may not to another. Those at different soul ages, for example, have different perspectives and lessons. In fact, we each have a different self-chosen curriculum. We might see someone's choices leading to unnecessary pain, but it's hard to know for sure what serves someone else's highest good. The pain they create might be inevitable at their current state of consciousness. It could lead to much growth. It may, in fact, have been part of their life plan. In any case, we can only choose for ourselves. Focusing on our own choices and leaving others alone is generally a good choice!

Often, many possible choices are pretty equal in terms of probable outcomes. Job A might have a different set of pros and cons than Job B, but when they're all added up, they might have similar tallies. And there might not be an ideal or "perfect" choice in a given situation. Simply making the best choice we can at least keeps us moving forward so that new choices can present themselves.

There is a saying that "You create your own reality from your core beliefs." Our core beliefs shape our energy, thoughts, and feelings, which influence our choices, which largely create our reality. For example, we will make different choices if we believe that the world is against us than if we believe that the world supports us, and different life experiences will result.

ALL IS CHOICE

We all have some negative, false core beliefs that limit us, many of which we are unaware. Becoming aware of them and changing them to be in alignment with truth can considerably accelerate our growth and improve our life. There are many techniques for accessing, exploring, and shifting our core beliefs directly. We can also change them from the outside in by being more aware of our choices and making them more from positive, true beliefs. For example, we can choose to act from the premise that we live in a benevolent, abundant universe even if we don't yet feel it.

True beliefs, those that are in harmony with the larger universe, are based in love and are naturally positive and constructive. There is much negativity in humanity, and we don't benefit from being in Pollyanna-ish denial of that. However, improving life on earth requires that we reach outside the closed system of human negativity and bring in the fresh air of universal love, truth, and beauty that are the basis of life.

For those on a spiritual path, the essential question when considering a choice is whether it is aligned with love, truth, and beauty and serves the highest good. This principle is the spiritual half of choice-making, and it is relatively simple and straightforward when we have a clear sense of what those qualities look and feel like. However, the material half—its application—is complex. A person can be purely loving in intention and still blunder through life. Practical considerations are specific to each situation. Mastering the art of living is an endless task that demands a great deal of knowledge, insight, experience, and skill. We live in a complicated, everchanging world, and there is always more to learn about it to enable increasingly better choices. We practice the art of living by making choices over many lifetimes.

2 • THE LIMITS OF REALITY CREATION

It's true that we do, in general, create our own reality. Our beliefs help generate our overall consciousness and resulting energy, which magnetizes things that resonate with it—like attracts like. Love attracts love, contention attracts contention, and so forth. Our energy attracts behavior in others: people with a chip on their shoulder tend to trigger combative behavior in others, whereas those with a sunny disposition tend to attract friendliness.

Our life is full of clues as to what underlying beliefs we carry because it is what we are creating from them. It is especially wise to examine repetitive negative patterns in our life. They can reveal frozen old beliefs that would be profitable to release.

However, others are also creating their reality, and their choices can affect us. In addition, sometimes things happen unexpectedly. The universe is only half structure and planning; the other half is chaos and surprise. Virulent diseases spread. Defects can arise that were not initially seen. People can choose not to keep soul-level agreements they made with us. Worse, people can choose to form karma with us. Karma is a major violation of another person that limits their choices, resulting in a compelling debt. Murder is one example. Part of the art of living is learning to stay out of the way of karma creators as much as possible.

Michael speaks of the scathing of the physical plane. Shit happens. Nearly everyone who lives long enough will experience ill health, financial challenges, and all the other negative things that accompany being human. Growing through joy implies being as skillful as possible and keeping them to a minimum, but no one eliminates them entirely. All souls are traumatized from time to time when we encounter stresses that we are not yet equipped to handle; by reviewing those experiences and healing the trauma, we become stronger. Maybe the next time we encounter something similar, we will be better equipped, having become wiser and more skilled, and will therefore get through it without being traumatized.

Even though we don't create everything that happens to us, we always have enough choice in regard to everything that happens to make a difference in our experience.

In the most limited circumstances, we still have choice as to how we frame and interpret them. If we do so more positively, we will have a more positive experience. It is always wise to endeavor to make the best of every situation and grow from it as much as possible. It is freeing to know that our internal experience isn't inevitable, that we have some control over how we respond. When external events trigger us, we can explore what needs healing or evolving in us so that such things don't trigger us in the future.

3 • OBSERVING OUR THOUGHTS

There's a maxim, "Don't believe everything you think (or feel)." In fact, being at least a little skeptical of all thoughts, our own and those of others, can serve us well. Being conscious implies that we step back and observe our thoughts and feelings. Are they true and loving? Do they make sense? What are their underlying beliefs? Are those beliefs consistent with our highest understanding? If not, we can make adjustments.

Many of us on a spiritual/personal growth path feel frustrated by the gap between the truths we resonate with and our day-to-day experience. "I know I shouldn't let this bother me, but ...." One usually starts with understanding, and it can gradually integrate into experience through ongoing spiritual practice and inner work. Peacefully holding the tension between our higher-self knowing and our lower-self conditioning can power the imprinting of our knowing into our lower self. The goal isn't to eliminate or repress the more negative parts of self but to elevate and integrate them.

Each personality has several subpersonalities such as our inner child and inner critic. Hearing and working with these can be a key to such integration. Modalities such as EFT (Emotional Freedom Technique), Journeywork, and many others can aid us in releasing blocks so that we feel and experience life in a more positive way. Working with a skilled, empathetic practitioner or therapist can give us tools we can use on our own as we gain proficiency. Well-being results when all parts of self are integrated and freely participate in choice-making.

4 • REASON

Everything in the universe is intelligent, and contributes to its creativity and evolution in its own way. Different beings play different "games" because they have their own purposes and lessons. Humans are what Michael refers to as "sentient souls" or "creatures of reason." (The other fully sentient species on Earth are the cetaceans—dolphins and whales.) That means that we are equipped to operate out of the intellectual part of our intellectual center. In the Michael teachings, centers are one of the overleaves (personality traits). The intellectual part of the intellectual center is the seat of pure reason. Reason is "the power of the mind to form judgments by a process of logic." Animals have an intellectual center—they have thoughts and opinions, and can do some simple strategizing. However, they do not reason; they don't analyze or plan, for instance—the intellectual part of their intellectual center isn't activated. They don't have self-awareness in the sense of thinking about themselves in a big-picture way. Many human beings don't take much advantage of that capacity, but it's there.

Our evolution isn't just intellectual, but skillful choice-making does have a strong intellectual component. It involves seeing and weighing options, anticipating possible consequences, and wisely deciding for more than short-term gain. Good choices rely on a clear, accurate grasp of facts, and the ability to put them in context and see their meaning, which is truth. The more we do this, the more our consciousness expands—we become conscious of more.

For most of human history, the majority of people have been largely unconscious and have resisted waking up. Michael refers to this as the "waking sleep." Another way of saying this is that the majority have most of the time resisted making conscious choices, which implies taking responsibility for our lives and reality creation. Although this is still the case, we are in the beginning stage of a collective awakening. How far this goes and how long it takes will, of course, be a matter of our collective choice.

One result of the waking sleep is that we have tended to embrace inaccurate information when it suits our biases or simply because we were inculcated with it. Being asleep, we haven't had sufficient discernment, curiosity, and love of truth to gain new and more accurate knowledge—we have been dull. This has hampered our growth of consciousness. The current cult of fake news and public disregard for facts and reason are especially damaging, but at least there is more awareness that this disinformation exists—it always has, although not always as brazenly as it currently is in many quarters.

Most of us value accurate information when it comes to making important purchases, for example. We probably don't want to buy a car that turns out to be a lemon, even if we like its styling. It may not always be clear what is accurate, but if we do our best to objectively research, we have a good chance of making a wise choice. However, when it comes to areas where we have ideologies, we lower the bar. Ideologies foster intellectual laziness: we just buy into them and no longer feel the need to think—most matters are already settled. Choices are decided by the ideology rather than by engaging with the specific, unique facts of a situation and bringing compassion and wisdom to them.

This too ultimately can be a lesson and lead to growth—we can see what happens when we act from false information. Eventually, we might embrace truth because we realize that it works better, that it leads to more pleasant results. It is common sense (sorely lacking in many) that we get better results when we have good information in every aspect of life, including medicine, politics, and religion. Although there are steps that can be taken to reduce the spread of disinformation, the ultimate answer is for us to love truth more, and to inspire a love of truth in others through our example. Embracing truth is in the enlightened self-interest of all. Only false personality (ego) prefers falsehoods.

Thought is meant to be fluid and alive. However, rigid thought forms are in the energetic atmosphere around us, ready to be downloaded and reinforced by those whose unresolved emotions resonate with them. They were created by all those who thought them before, without much awareness. Ideologies are strings of them. Rigidity inhibits the growth of consciousness. We benefit enormously from releasing thought forms and ideologies in favor of direct nuanced observation and knowing.

Growth is not only having experiences, but learning from them. We will probably eventually learn something from most of our experiences, but mileage varies, as they say. A quote I love is that "Some people have fifty years of experience, while others have one year of experience fifty times." The latter are trapped in a maze, a closed system, from which only awakening can free them.

Another result of the waking sleep is drawing incorrect conclusions from experiences. A common example is when we have a bad experience with someone, and then form a prejudice against everyone who happens to share a common trait, whether it be gender, race, religion, sexual orientation, or anything else. The subconscious is not rational. We all want to be treated as the individual we are rather than be classified generically. The Golden Rule suggests that we extend that courtesy to others. However, our subconscious dumbly uses these generalizations to avoid having more pain in the future. Only by bringing the light of consciousness to bear can we avoid this trap and recognize precisely what brought us pain in the bad experience. (Hint: It might have been us.) Prejudice is unreasonable, and true reason can help us release it, although negative programming can require some work to clear.

Much therapy is concerned with discovering the incorrect conclusions we drew, especially as children, and correcting them. For example, some of us concluded, "It's my fault!" when our parents fought. We therefore developed some dysfunctional ways of being, trying to compensate for that. "It's my fault!" is an example of a thought form that can attract several others that link together and throw us off track.

Past-life therapy can help us recognize faulty conclusions we drew in past lives that are still coloring our choices now, so that we are freer to make new choices.

The ability to recognize what love actually looks and feels like is our best tool in this work. It is the yardstick against which we can measure our thoughts and feelings to see whether they hold water. Love and truth are inextricably linked. Inevitably, unloving thoughts are not truly reasonable.

5 • SELF-VALIDATION

Like choice, self-validation is a core concept of the Michael teachings. It means that we don't take someone else's word for things but test them in our experience and make the knowledge our own. For example, when people receive their channeled Michael Reading chart, if they just accept it without validating it, the information isn't very useful. If someone tells me that I'm a sage soul, that's nice. If I learn what that means in depth and then compare that with my experience of myself, I will either see the truth of it or I will contest it. I can then try other *roles* (soul types) on for size and see whether they fit me better. I may actually be a sage but decide that I'm a king, perhaps because of secondary chart influences that I don't understand. Deciding that doesn't make it so, but at least I am engaging in the process and have a chance to eventually achieve clarity. I can then profitably use the knowledge in my daily life. Knowledge that isn't self-won is just theory.

6 • PREDICTIONS

Relying too much on psychics and channels before making decisions can weaken our choice-making "muscles." They might be able to help us better consider our options, but some people look to them to predict the future before making a choice. Good choices don't depend on predicting the future. In fact, they cannot, because no one has ever actually predicted the future. Some people are adept at reading probabilities—where things are currently heading—but probabilities can change based on the choices people make and unforeseen events. We all have free will and there is a great deal of chaos. We have to make choices based on what makes the most sense to us and what feels right, not knowing for sure what others will do or what the future will bring. If we don't yet have clarity, we aren't done processing our thoughts and feelings. Perhaps we need to do more research.

That said, what feels right to us may include our sense of probabilities. People with well-developed intuition have their ear to the ground and can sense things that are in the process of occurring but haven't yet manifested. In 1999, a friend was becoming increasingly uneasy with her and her husband's stock market investments and begged him to get out, but he refused. He didn't trust her famous female intuition. They lost almost everything when the tech bubble burst. This was different from going to a psychic and being told to get out of the market. It was a strong, visceral feeling, not merely intellectual. It is worth considering the advice of others, including psychics and channels, but it should be weighed by our own intuition: "Is this a feeling that I'd also been having but hadn't trusted or previously made conscious? Or does it feel off?" Also consider the psychic's track record, if possible. However, even those with good track records are wrong fairly often. Many people have been burned by blindly taking such advice. We need to use all our faculties to make wise choices.

7 • THE ROLE OF FEELING

What we feel emotionally and in our body can contribute to good choice-making, guiding us away from choices that seem logical and supported by facts but are, in fact, misguided. Making choices that deeply feel wrong to us, despite what others say or what our mind tells us, is likely to lead to regrets. Our body and emotions are plugged in to sources of information that our intellect isn't. For example, our body may tell us that someone who seems perfectly nice and straightforward is lying, or at least that something is off. The caveat is that "gut feelings" that don't go deep enough may just be our biases or fear at work, which can lead to poor choices.

Emotions have tended to get a bad rap. When people act irrationally, they are said to be acting emotionally. However, emotions can be rational, and intellect can be irrational. Reason alone, not balanced with true feeling, has many pitfalls and can lead to faulty conclusions. For one thing, reason depends on starting with correct assumptions. The real issue with both intellect and emotion is whether unexamined biases are controlling them. Some people are naturally more intellectual, but that doesn't mean that they are necessarily seeing facts more clearly and honestly, and are therefore making better choices. Even scientists and journalists with high integrity and intelligence, who work hard to be objective, have at least some biases that interfere with their perceptions. It is impossible to be completely bias-free. Still, it behooves us to endeavor to have greater self-

7 • THE ROLE OF FEELING

awareness of our biases. Biases are frozen, distorted beliefs from the past that keep us from engaging with the present in a fresh, clear way. Operating with fewer biases can improve all our experiences, whether we're a journalist, artist, or businessperson.

Being balanced is a key to life. Those who are more intellectual can benefit from being in greater touch with their emotions and body so that they don't live in their head. Those who are more emotional might want to strengthen their reasoning capacities, and exercise might make them feel better. People who are highly physical can become more effective by developing their mind and emotions more.

We get the best results in choice-making when we use all our faculties in unity, receiving input not only from all parts of our personality—mind, emotions, and body—but also from our higher self (essence) and guides. Then our choices can be aligned with our life path and highest good, and we can find knowing "in our bones." Input from other people, the internet, and other sources of information can also be helpful.

8 • PRIORITIES

We can do everything we want to do—just not all at the same time. Eventually, we will have enough lifetimes to do everything that strongly interests us. One of the reasons that the lower (concrete) planes of creation have the linearity of time is so that we can focus on one thing at a time, in sequence. A big element of choice is choosing what the highest priority is now, and now, and now. On the higher (abstract) planes, things are experienced more as being simultaneous. Being relatively inexperienced, we as souls are not yet ready to handle that complexity.

On the physical plane, it is impossible to do more than one thing with our body at the same time. Multitasking is simply switching back and forth among various activities, maybe stirring a pot on the stove, then tending to a child, then putting the laundry into the dryer, and then back to the stove. Four of the seven essence roles, *artisan, sage, priest,* and *server*, have more than one input (psychic receptors) but they still only have one output—they still only do one physical thing at a time. True, we can talk on the phone while washing dishes since washing dishes may not require a lot of attention and we probably don't need to physically do much with the phone. But none of us can wash dishes while vacuuming the carpet—we have to choose one or the other.

If we choose to do one thing in this moment, we are choosing not to do several others. If I choose to go to bed later because I am reading online articles, I am also choosing to either get less sleep or to wake up later. Getting less sleep might mean feeling less well. Waking up later might mean not doing other things. Every choice has ramifications. We may try to ignore them but we still have to live with them, so we may as well engage with them. Many of us resist prioritizing because we want to do what we want to do in the moment, and don't want to face the consequences. We get points for realizing that we are resisting making a conscious choice when it is happening, even if we don't muster the control to overcome our resistance.

Self-discipline is often thought of as making ourselves do things we don't want to do because they are good for us. It might be more useful to instead frame it as being more conscious of our choices: Would I rather stay up later and have less sleep, or would I rather stop doing what I'm doing and get more? The latter may require overcoming inertia, but it is good work to become more conscious of our choices and not let inertia make them for us.

9 • CONSCIOUSLY CHOOSING

Not making a choice is also a choice, but a passive one, one that doesn't own our personal power but surrenders it to circumstances or the choices of others.

We also make many choices, perhaps most of them, unconsciously We can't be aware of every choice, but expanding consciousness implies that more of our choices are becoming conscious, and therefore *we* are becoming more conscious.

An example is breathing. We mostly breathe without making a conscious choice to do so, fortunately. However, many of us have poor breathing habits. Being conscious of them can help us improve them. We can practice better habits until they become second nature. They again become unconscious but improved because we brought the light of consciousness to bear on them.

We make many unconscious choices in the realm of energy. Most people are not even aware that they have an energy field, so it is impossible for them to make conscious choices relative to it. Still, it has a potent impact on our well-being. I wrote a short book on this subject, *Energy Literacy*. An example is *cording*, which refers to attaching energy suckers to others and/or letting others attach them to us. We may unconsciously allow that because we want to be needed by them, or feel that we owe it to them. We may cord others because we feel weak and they seem strong. Expanding our consciousness so that we're aware of our energy field empowers us to make better choices about such things. In this example, if we release cords in both directions (other than with our young children, which is what cording is intended for), our well-being increases.

When we react to others without thinking, without consciously choosing our words and actions, we are more likely to become enmeshed in their energy, losing our spiritual freedom. When we slow down a bit and consider our choices, we can bring our higher understanding to bear. Choosing from love, we can be helpful, perhaps defusing a fraught situation rather than escalating tensions.

People often explode in anger, causing pain to others. The only alternative seems to be repressing it, causing pain to self. Knowing that what we do with our anger (and other feelings) is a choice might be little comfort to those who try to control it but find that they can't. The most effective domain of choice here lies in taking advantage of calm moments to explore and work with the sources of our anger and bring healing before it gets to the point of exploding. Gaining a sophisticated understanding of how to release stored energies such as anger is highly useful to everyone on a spiritual path. There are many excellent therapeutic techniques such as pounding pillows and psychodrama, but a simple and potent one is to sit quietly and feel the anger without commentary until it burns off.

10 • BLAMING THE VICTIMS

Those who misunderstand reality creation and choice sometimes believe that people who experience misfortune chose it, and that helping them interferes with their choice. They believe that on a soul level, others wanted to experience poverty, ill health, or whatever. That is not the case. We are all in this together. If we were born into more fortunate circumstances, our lessons could revolve around learning to help those who have less rather than coldly standing idly by.

There are many reasons souls choose their parents and circumstances. For one thing, there are not many privileged ones available, and there are compromises involved in every choice. A family abundant in money may be scarce in love. Being born into monetary wealth is not a reward for good karma, as some believe. We tend to incarnate with souls we knew in past lives, especially those who are members of our *entity* (soul family), *cadre* (seven entities) and *cadre group* or *energy ring* (twelve cadres). It varies, but on average, we tend to mostly interact with about three hundred souls in various capacities from lifetime to lifetime. Maybe our "gang" has tended to incarnate in the Western world, which on the whole is currently more prosperous. If our parents happen to be wealthy in this lifetime, that may in fact be immaterial to why we chose them (and they chose us). Instead, there could be karmic reasons, for example, or certain lessons we wanted to work on together. Similarly, for those who incarnate into poverty, the poverty might have been immaterial. We tend to overrate the importance of wealth and comfort to the soul (although no one would dispute that having more materially is nice).

11 • THE KARMIC WHEEL

Increasing others' choices is "good work" and can create philanthropic karma. Decreasing others' choices can create negative karma, which entangles us with others and pulls us off the spiritual path. It keeps us on the karmic wheel, as Hinduism puts it. Those on a conscious spiritual path seek to get off the karmic wheel, which we cannot do when we are too invested in others' choices. (I write "*conscious* spiritual path" because everyone is actually on a spiritual path, but most don't know it or actively pursue it. Which is their choice. ☺) Minding our own business is not only good for others; it is good for us, too. It both helps keep us out of draining entanglements and gives us more energy to focus on our own choices, making it more likely that we'll make better ones.

Michael's teachings about choice are not moral relativism, as in "My opinion of what is right and wrong is just as good as yours." The idea of moral relativism comes from observing the vastly different ideas about right and wrong in different cultures. Dietary restrictions vary among religions. Some believe that dancing on Sunday is wrong (and you'll go to hell if you do it). Many societies believe that some addictive substances are wrong and others are okay, but what goes on which list varies and can change. We may choose to follow the rules to avoid getting into trouble. We may even choose to believe that these rules accurately represent right and wrong, but they are often arbitrary and tend to create unhappiness. Michael teaches that all choices are

11 • THE KARMIC WHEEL

valid in the sense that we can learn from all of them, but they aren't saying that all choices are equally skillful or positive. We have the right to make any choice, including to form karma, but we do pay the consequences. Others also have the right to try to stop us. Of course, those on a spiritual path wish to be a force for good.

Actual right and wrong are intrinsic in energy: If one violates another person or the environment, doing harm, that automatically creates karma. No one has to (or gets to) decide that, because the energy will compel a resolution if there is an actual violation. If we choose to create karma, we are choosing to "grow through pain" by living with the karma we have created and may thereby learn a lesson. Michael encourages their students to instead "grow through joy," which is making reasoned choices that serve the greatest good.

Of course, one would prefer that humanity made wiser choices that create less suffering, The Michael teachings don't condone karma creation; they just point out the fact of it and teach how to more skillfully navigate the physical plane as it is. It's good to do all that we effectively can to help, shining our light and using positive persuasion whenever possible. But then we need to let go of what we have no power over if we are to maintain our sanity.

12 • IT'S ALL GOOD

We don't choose *everything* in our lives, but we choose the lion's share, or at least the majority springs from other choices we made, even if unintended. We had a pretty good idea before incarnating what our situation would be during at least the first few years of life, although there's always the possibility of unexpected changes.

The soul is more interested in growth and creativity than in having everything be pleasant and easy—we need challenges to grow. Pleasant and easy incarnations aren't easy to come by, anyway. The things that happen to us that we did not choose (for example, someone else choosing to create karma with us) still give us opportunities to be resourceful in solving problems and overcoming obstacles. So, as they say, it's all good.

Choices are never unlimited, and we all at least sometimes find ourselves in situations in which our choices are curbed by the excessive dominance of others or institutions. We grow by challenging ourselves to make the best possible choices among those that are available, even when they are severely limited; we always have at least some. It is a good idea to consider our range of choices with as much calm and objectivity as we can.

One of the greatest hindrances to our spiritual growth is not recognizing the full scope of our choices—how many choices are actually available to make—and therefore, how powerful we really are. When there seem to be few good options, sometimes an increase of creativity in our problem-solving can reveal others. These include those not just in the physical world but also in the spiritual/energetic realms. An example is addressing health problems through energy work in addition to what doctors offer. Thinking outside the box can lead to an expansion of consciousness. Sometimes, others who are not as invested as we are can make good suggestions. Research and brainstorming can expand our awareness of possibilities and can help expand our consciousness in general. Being creative in our problem-solving is an important part of becoming better creators in general.

Consciousness expands in two ways: horizontally and vertically. Horizontal (sideways) expansion increases our awareness of our world. Vertical expansion, of the unseen higher and lower realms. Both are valuable. Psychic development exercises could help with the latter.

Part II

WHAT WE HAVE THE RIGHT TO CHOOSE

13 • INCARNATIONAL CHOICE

A key aspect of "All is choice" is that on some level, we chose to be here. As eternal sparks of the Tao, we chose the kind of essence we would use to experience Earth (one of seven roles) and our entity, or soul family. As souls, we chose where and when we would be born, our parents, personality, etc. If we were born by c-section, we still agreed to accept the time of birth as part of the package. There may have been things about our parents and body that were not ideal, but we also accepted them as part of the package that seemed, on the whole, right for our purposes. We generally make our parent/child agreement with either the mother or father; perhaps that soul then mated with someone who was not great for our purposes. We had the option to back out of the agreement and find another parent. Since we didn't, that demonstrates that we also accepted the other parent, again, as part of the package. Sometimes the choice of parent or childhood circumstances isn't that consequential. Being born through *someone* allowed us to be here, playing the learning game that is human life on Earth.

Some people bitterly proclaim that they didn't choose to be born. The majority of people are in false (fear-based) personality, or ego, which is cut off from essence, our true self. It's true that false personality didn't choose to be born. However, as we awaken to our eternal nature, we realize that we did, in fact, choose to be born, again and again! "All is choice."

14 • GOVERNMENT

An implication of the Michael teachings is that giving people maximum freedom over the choices that are rightly theirs to make is most in harmony with the universe and what we're here to learn. Michael isn't political, but in the sense of having respect for the free will of individuals, they are among the most libertarian of spiritual teachers.

Each person has the right to choose anything that doesn't infringe on the choices of others. Wiccans correctly teach, "An' it harm none, do what ye will." Determining where the line is, however, can be tricky, and legal systems are forever trying to sort that out. What constitutes direct material harm to others?

Do people have the right to play loud music when others are trying to sleep or enjoy quiet? Probably not, although some will protest their right to do so. Those of good will can often work these things out. In this example, people might wear headphones to listen to the music they want. Maybe that seems like a slight inconvenience, but to live peaceably with others, it is important not to just claim our own perceived rights but to also be considerate of the needs of others. On the other hand, if neighbors are having a rare loud party, we can wear earplugs.

Certainly, the right to choose includes sovereignty over our own body. Applying that to government suggests that most laws concerning drugs and abortion would be eliminated. This is an area that illustrates the futility of trying to control the personal choices of others. The war on drugs has been a costly failure that has led to a great increase in crime. Women have long sought abortions regardless of laws, but die much more often from them when they are illegal.

Drug abuse does have a cost to society, and governments are within their rights to regulate their distribution, making sure that they are not adulterated and that people have good information on them, fully understanding the risks. It is a benefit to society to provide those who become addicted with rehabilitation if they wish to have it. However, people have taken mind-altering drugs since the beginning and will always be curious about them regardless of laws. Sometimes they are used for valuable spiritual and healing purposes.

Societies only thrive when there is safety and order. Enforcing reasonable boundaries such as preventing murders and separating those who commit them from society, ideally attempting to rehabilitate them, is an intelligent use of governments. So is protecting the environment, and many other things. The governments that humans create and the scope of their power are part of collective choice. All choices lead to results, and if we're wise, we observe them and learn to make more skillful choices in the future.

There is at least some injustice in most governments, in addition to the many things that one might simply disagree with. A certain amount of that falls into the domain of social contract, meaning that this is how the collective has chosen to do things. If it isn't egregious or hypocritical, it may not create karma. There can be good sense in accepting the local social contract as part of the package of where we choose or need to live. It allows us to focus on our life with fewer distractions. It can also be a positive choice to disobey it, perhaps drawing attention to inequities, but the consequences of that are also part of the package. Humanity is still mentally and emotionally primitive, and expecting enlightenment from governments is likely to lead to disappointment. As humanity evolves, institutions such as governments are usually the last to change to reflect new consciousness, being at the outer layer of societies.

Freedom is often claimed in the service of egoic selfishness, as in "I'm gonna do what I want, and nobody is going to tell me otherwise!" Political libertarianism also claims this right for corporations. When taken to extremes, this leads to an inability to cooperate for the common good, often producing harm to all, such as allowing pollution that creates climate change. "Balance in all things" is a good credo. For the spiritual seeker, freedom is seen as a gift not to be squandered but claimed in service to humanity and spiritual growth.

Our collective reality, the world we live in, is the result of all the previous choices humanity has made. The results of elections, etc., are collective choices. It's true that the system can be set up in biased, distorted ways so that each person doesn't have an equal say (or any say) but that system is still a collective creation, a reflection of the consciousness of those there and those who came before. Even unjust systems may have many supporters who believe that they are right or inevitable, simply how things are done. If the rich and powerful have stacked the decks in their favor (as they always have), it's obviously because they started with more resources. Still, those who accept the status quo contribute to its maintenance; it cannot stand without mass cooperation. If there's enough will, the collective can change the system, especially in putative democracies, although it's not always easy. So "All is choice" applies. The collective reality may not be what we personally would like, but we chose it as part of our incarnational package.

Even when policies or those elected do not reflect the wishes of the majority, those who support them get to experience the results of their beliefs and wishes, which can lead to their growth. Those who oppose them also get to see what happens down that particular path, and that can also be growthful, if frustrating. Michael often says that no experience is wasted; we need experiences to process in order to grow. These will inevitably include negative ones to some degree.

15 • RELIGION

Many religions and spiritual teachings believe that the highest path is blind obedience to their idea of God and its rules, and/or to the pastor, guru, or other leader supposedly representing God. It is rare for any to teach the sanctity of choice. God's ways are said to be inscrutable. According to them, we are to forever remain God's young children, never understanding or taking responsibility for creating our life, never growing up into spiritual adults. If we're lucky, we get to play a harp near God's throne or something after we die.

Especially when we're spiritually young and not as capable of making wise choices, we can benefit from guidance from those who are more experienced and far-seeing. However, it is said that good teachers make themselves progressively unnecessary. In the classic guru/disciple relationship that has been traditional in India for centuries, this does not happen. Disciples are expected to unquestioningly do what their gurus tell them, often with little explanation. Later, they may become gurus themselves. When do they ever learn to discern and make choices (other than the choice to obey or not)?

Ram Dass told of his beloved guru Maharajji (Neem Karoli Baba) instructing him to stop having sex with a man that he had been delighted to have finally found. Throughout much of history, most religious and spiritual groups have been woefully ignorant about sexuality and staunchly anti-gay. Although one cannot know Maharajji's motivation, cultural homophobia seems likely to have been part of it. Maharajji also told him to give away his large inheritance; when Ram Dass became ill late in life and had no money, there were extensive fund-raising efforts on his behalf.

Maybe abstaining from sex with that man and giving his money away were positive, wise choices and best aided Ram Dass's growth; maybe not. Maybe they were only right according to that culture's belief systems but not actually for Ram Dass's highest good. Had Maharajji suggested rather than dictated, giving his reasoning and using it as a teaching opportunity, at least the choices would have been Ram Dass's. He could have tried different scenarios on for size, seeing what felt right. Maybe he would have tried a non-sexual relationship with this man and noticed the results of that, either deciding that it worked better for him or that it didn't. Maybe the idea of giving away his inheritance would have felt liberating, or maybe what felt best would have been to give away part and keep part. Maybe he would have kept it all but without attachment, using it for worthwhile projects. Deciding for himself, he would have been able to make a correlation between his choices and the consequences; he would have been more empowered.

There is no indication that Ram Dass later objected to his guru's dictates; he assumed their rightness. Maybe giving up his will was part of his path of growth. The idea behind submitting to the guru is that it helps dissolve the ego, or self. However, it did not aid him in becoming more skillful at choice-making, which, according to Michael, is a big part of why we're here.

Michael teaches that the goal is to gradually release false personality but not the personality itself. False personality is the personality distorted by fear, whereas true personality springs from love and accurately reflects aspects of essence, our eternal nature. Personality is as valid as essence. The point is for personality and essence to work in harmony, not to destroy personality. Ideally, personality is in a state of relaxed nonattachment, as Buddhists put it. That means making the best choices we are capable of, moment after moment, letting the results take care of themselves without trying to manipulate them. That is integrity: doing the right, wise thing simply because it is right and wise, letting the chips fall where they may. Essence created personality in order to have experiences on the physical plane. It is not meant to be destroyed; it is meant to be operated consciously, in love. In its positive poles, personality is not a hindrance but a unique vessel for essence.

In any case, dissolving the ego doesn't work. People who claim that they have or at least try to tend to be dysfunctional. There is a lot of evidence that even gurus capable of doing amazing things are not always in integrity. There are many stories of them abusing their power to sexually or financially take advantage of their disciples, for example. Their tradition doesn't include much psychological sophistication, so there is not a lot of self-analysis. Like cult leaders and the pope, gurus are viewed as being infallible, so it can be confusing when their faults come to light.

ALL IS CHOICE

Many evangelical Christians unquestioningly believe that abortion is the same as murdering babies, that the moment a sperm fertilizes an egg, that is a baby. The appeal of such an absolutist ideology may be that it eliminates any gray area, any need to discern when a developing fetus becomes a person. (Progressives generally define personhood as being capable of functioning outside the womb.) However, a zygote is .006 inches. Comparing that to a baby seems far-fetched. Even after three months, a fetus only weighs one ounce. Where did the evangelicals' idea come from? The Bible doesn't mention abortion, so clearly, some previous church officials somehow came to this conclusion and started teaching it. Others unquestioningly adopted that view, and the emotionally charged ideology spread and became entrenched. The belief that a one-ounce fetus is a person is used to justify interfering with a woman's right to choose what happens in her body. The point here isn't to argue abortion, but it should be said that women don't undertake abortions lightly and would likely only get a later-term abortion if there are grave issues of health at stake. Nobody wants to murder babies. This lightning rod issue isn't real—it's made up—and distracts from real issues such as poverty and climate change.

Similar to this is the Catholic idea that using birth control interferes with the will of God but that other medical interventions such as surgery or pills do not. Some human beings arbitrarily decided that and imposed it on others. One suspects ulterior motives, such as wanting Catholics to have large families in order to increase their numbers (and finances). The

15 • RELIGION

core idea is that only the infallible pope can know the will of God, and that no one else has the right to choose. Fortunately, many Catholics cherry-pick from among the rules and ignore those that don't suit them, although that might be accompanied by guilt. At least they can have it absolved through confession. Their version of God is forgiving if they eventually play by the rules.

16 • GUIDES

Those of us who have developed the ability to consciously communicate with our spirit guides and teachers, or who receive channeling or readings from those who have, may believe that if guidance comes from Spirit (with a capital S), it is infallible. Therefore, we should blindly follow it. Some guides might themselves believe that. It's true that they have access to information that we don't and may be able to be more objective than we are, but they can be wrong, too. Our guides are our friends; like our human friends, they don't always give great advice. They are usually at a similar level development to our own—we may have previously been *their* guides. They are learning valuable skills by guiding us. They are highly familiar with what we ourselves planned for this lifetime, and they coach us from the sidelines to try to help us keep our eye on the ball. However, sometimes things change and we need to adjust our plans. We are not bound to our original plan and always maintain the right to choose.

I've been communicating with my guides daily for over forty years. I've found that they prove to be correct about ninety percent of the time, sometimes uncannily so, as in "How on earth did they know *that*?" But they can be wrong, sometimes distressingly so, about ten percent of the time. I've gotten a feel for the types of guidance I am less likely to agree with. An example is shopping advice. They enjoy going shopping with me (they didn't have Costco in their last lifetime) and I appreciate their opinions, but have learned to make my own decisions.

Every being on every plane of creation is evolving and is therefore fallible. There is a valuable loss of innocence in realizing that all are fallible, similar to realizing as we grew up that our parents are fallible. We can learn to become comfortable and feel safe in a universe where nothing is guaranteed or foolproof. Life is a game of learning and creativity, and nothing is static.

Each of us is responsible for our own choices. We have to live with their consequences, and it does us no good to blame whoever suggested a particular course of action, including our guides. When we made the choice, it was ours. It's empowering to own all our choices. Michael teaches that there are no wrong choices because we can learn from all of them. Certainly there are choices we regret, but we can be thankful for the lessons and move on. We can only do our best; if we do that consistently, our best will get better.

There are times when it is good to follow spiritual guidance even when we cannot see the reason for it or it doesn't make sense intellectually, especially if it's coming through with particular strength and clarity. We may discover later just how right-on it was; it might even save our life. However, all things need checks and balances. Communication with our guides is mostly intellectual. Feel into it: if it feels okay, then why not follow it, especially if there is little to lose? If we've put aside our fear and biases, and it still feels wrong, it might be better to pass on it.

Michael is the rare teacher who aims to empower their students, including to help them make better choices on their own rather than relying on Michael. They rarely tell their students what to do, but help them gain clarity about their situation and options.

17 • CHOOSING OUR WORDS

Some people admire those who speak without filters, seeing them as being real and honest, perhaps brutally so. But like ideologies, this is also laziness. They are not evaluating what would be most helpful to the situation or considering other people's feelings. They are not thinking. They are just allowing their id ("the primitive and instinctual part of the mind that contains aggressive drives and hidden memories") to explode. They aren't making conscious choices; they are letting their subconscious choose. Self-serving lies and unexamined, unprocessed thoughts and feelings from the past may spew out helter-skelter.

This choice to let the subconscious choose results in a degradation of one's vibration and influences others downward, whereas well-chosen words uplift.

Part III

WHAT WE DON'T HAVE THE RIGHT TO CHOOSE

18 • OTHERS' RIGHT TO CHOOSE

If we have the right to choose, other people also have the right to make their own choices. We generally don't have the right to interfere with those that affect only themselves. In any case, we've probably observed how futile it usually is to try to change others, although that doesn't stop us from trying. We certainly have the right to offer help or to express our concerns or preferences. It's fine to share how their choices make us feel. It's also within our rights to disconnect from a relationship or situation that is not working for us. However, it's not legitimate to try to force others to make the decisions we think they should. When we try to control others, we become entangled with them, which leads to all sort of problems. (See my book *Energy Literacy*.)

In relationships, if one person wants to do one thing and the other wants to do something different, a solution might lie in realizing that they don't have to always do the same things, that they can each do what they wish and do things together when their wishes overlap.

Inner peace gives us more energy to effectively act. We waste a great deal of energy trying to control others or railing against the choices they make, often those that they have the right to make. That takes us away from calmly focusing on our own reality creation in the present moment. When it comes to politics, that might include activism, voting, writing letters, etc., that can help persuade those in power to make better choices when they have the right to make them. When they do not, it might entail taking legal action. The universe allows everyone to make whatever choices they want—that's the definition of free will—but those who harm others and infringe on their right to choose in significant ways create karmic debts, which people on a spiritual path will want to avoid.

If someone is mentally impaired, we might temporarily impose aid to protect their safety so that they can live to make future choices, but that should be done sparingly. Forcing our will on others, depriving them of choices that are rightly theirs even if we think it's for their own good, can create karmic debts. It is frustrating and painful to see loved ones suffering, perhaps needlessly from our point of view. Still, we must be realistic about what we can do and what we have the right to do, although there is some gray area here. Having respect for their right to choose and the Golden Rule, putting ourselves in their place and asking how we might feel about the kind of interference we contemplate, can moderate our impulses.

19 • CHILDREN

It is appropriate for parents and other adults to make enough choices for children to keep them safe and from infringing on others. However, from the beginning, it's best if adults give children as much practice in making choices as possible. By the time they are in early adolescence, they should be making a majority of their own decisions. That allows them to see the ramifications of their choices and therefore learn how to make them more skillfully. I'm not suggesting permissiveness or a laissez-faire approach, but one that guides young people to explore what they chose and why; if they don't like the results, how might they have created different ones? It is unwise to try to protect children from every conceivable mistake, which is impossible anyway. Of course, protect them as much as possible from inflicting substantial harm on themselves and others, but micromanaging their lives weakens them and drives them away.

A choice-centered approach is likely to make for better relationships between parents and children. Many people carry resentment of their parents' excessive authoritarian force when raising them. It has been common throughout history for parents to be overly controlling and adversarial. This is something that more conscious people are beginning to question and change. Again, the Golden Rule applies. All too often, parents unconsciously inflict on their children the same kind of oppression that they resented when their parents inflicted it on them. The way to release our pictures of what parenting (or

19 • CHILDREN

anything else) looks like is to become more conscious of our choices, holding them up against our highest vision of unconditional love.

Let's say that you have a surly fifteen-year-old. If your approach to parenting hasn't been adversarial or heavy-handed, their natural rebellion probably won't be extreme, but every child is different and comes with their own issues. The quality of parenting that children receive is not the only factor in their behavior. In any case, blaming yourself isn't helpful, but if what you have been doing also hasn't been helpful, it's common sense to stop doing it. It's said that "The definition of insanity is doing the same thing over and over again and expecting different results."

We can observe this in all dysfunctional relationships: people repeating the same patterns that make each other miserable and failing to step outside of them to observe and change them. That takes becoming more conscious. To release the patterns, the first step would probably be to really listen to the other person.

I was fascinated to learn that a large percentage of teen athletes stop exercising regularly as soon as they don't have a coach bearing down on them. Joining the team might have initially been their choice, but from then on, their motivation comes from outside themselves. This illustrates why it's important to become self-motivated, to become aware of our choices and make them consciously. Even when we have mixed feelings about a choice—perhaps we felt pressured—we still get best results when we take ownership of our choices. For example, many teens don't like school but the law and/or their parents require that they attend. If they make the best of it and own their choice to go (rather than refusing), they will have a better experience.

20 • HIERACHIES

For those of us who work in a hierarchal company, our "boss," no matter how incompetent in our view, has the right to make some choices that affect us. We signed up for that by taking the job. Acceptance is necessary if we are to be at peace in the situation. On the other hand, using good communication skills with supervisors might persuade them that different choices might work better. The better we are at nonviolent communication (also called "compassionate" or "collaborative communication"), the higher our chances are of improving our situation, in all aspects of our life.

The coming decades should see an increase in less-hierarchal organizational structures where each person's voice is more welcome. We all can learn something from everyone, and it is in our best interest to be open to the ideas of others.

CONCLUSION

Focusing on the choices that are ours to make and withdrawing our attention from those that are not is liberating and our only path to peace of mind. As we choose to the best of our ability what is aligned with eternal love, truth, and beauty, and respect the right of others to make their own choices, we raise our vibration and become increasingly self-actualized.

ABOUT THE AUTHOR

SHEPHERD HOODWIN has been channeling since 1986. He also does intuitive readings, mediumship, past-life regression, healing, counseling, and channeling coaching (teaching others to channel). He has conducted workshops on the Michael teachings throughout the United States and Europe.

Shepherd is a graduate of the University of Oregon. He lives in Laguna Niguel, California.

https://shepherdhoodwin.com

TWITTER:
@shepherdh
@EnlightenNitwit

FACEBOOK:
https://www.facebook.com/shepherd.hoodwin
https://www.facebook.com/shepherd.hoodwin.author/
https://www.facebook.com/JourneyOfYourSoul/
https://www.facebook.com/EnlightenmentforNitwits/

shepherdhoodwin@gmail.com

Summerjoy Press
99 Pearl
Laguna Niguel CA 92677-4818

OTHER BOOKS BY SHEPHERD HOODWIN

Available at https://shepherdhoodwin.com/book/

Being in the World

This insightful book explores practical spirituality. Topics include aging, karma, time, and religion.

Compassion for Evil
A Metaphysical View

Compassion for Evil explores the nature of evil from the soul's point of view, and how we can skillfully deal with it as lightworkers.

Embracing What Is
Spiritual Keys to Happiness

This book is an abridged version of *Happiness and the Michael Teachings*, without technical Michael teachings terminology. A free version is available at Smashwords.com.

Energy Literacy
How to Perceive and Take Charge of Your Spiritual Well-Being

Energy Literacy is an introduction to how to perceive our energy field and release negativity. Topics include chakras, contracts, vows, cording, entities, implants, psychic attack, earthbound souls, soul retrieval, and more.

Enlightenment for Nitwits
The Complete Guide

This hilarious metaphysical/self-help humor collection will appeal to Oprah and Dave Barry fans as well as those with more esoteric interests. In a style reminiscent of comedian Steven Wright, it's full of wry one-liners along with longer, hilariously mind-bending pieces on a wide range of subjects, tied together by the idea of clueless humans trying to find enlightenment.

"I love *Enlightenment for Nitwits*! It is the funniest book I have read in several decades. If laughter leads to enlightenment, it will certainly do it. Nothing—thank God—is sacred in this delightful spoof on life in general."
—C. Norman Shealy, M.D., author of *Life Beyond 100*

Growing Through Joy

This thought-provoking book explores the nature of personal growth.

Happiness and the Michael Teachings
Learning to Embrace What Is

Happiness is the ultimate goal of every spiritual teaching. Here we explore several principles of what the Michael teachings refer to as growing through joy.

Healing the Gut
A Crib Sheet for Eliminating SIBO

This short ebook offers tips for those with digestive problems and related diseases, focusing on the Specific Carbohydrate Diet.

Journey of Your Soul
A Channel Explores the Michael Teachings

This is the most in-depth discussion of the Michael teachings to date. It may also be the first analytical study of channeling written by a channel. It has forewords by John Friedlander, author of *Psychic Psychology*, and Jon Klimo, author of *Channeling: Investigations on Receiving Information from Paranormal Sources*. Klimo writes, "*Journey of Your Soul* may well be the best (Michael) book of them all due to its clarity, thoroughness, and detail, and thanks to the fact that the author, an exceptionally clear-headed Michael channel himself, brings real integrity and authenticity to our understanding of Michael in particular and to the channeling process in general."

Loving from Your Soul
Creating Powerful Relationships

This inspiring, transformative book explores the nature of love itself as well as practical matters of relationships. One reader wrote, "There are phrases that are so inspiring that I wrote them down to refer to when I need them. I am looking forward to reading this book again and again."

Meditations for Self-Discovery
Guided Journeys for Communicating with Your Inner Self

This is a beautiful collection of forty-five vivid, often pastoral, guided imagery meditations channeled from Shepherd's essence. There are many meditation recordings available, but this is one of the first collections of meditations in book form that can be read to oneself or others. Teachers and group leaders would find it particularly useful.

Opening to Healing
This uplifting book explores the spiritual aspect of healing.

Unconditional Love in Politics
Or Have You Hugged a Republican/Democrat Today?

Is unconditional love in politics an oxymoron? Thus far, it's been a rare commodity if it's ever been there. This book explores what you can do about it, as well as why both right and left have useful parts to play in our evolution, the factors that influence a person's tilt to the right or left, and what unconditional love might look like in this sphere.

Why We're Attracted
Spiritual, Psychological and Physical Elements That

OTHER BOOKS BY SHEPHERD HOODWIN

Draw Us to Others

Just why are we attracted to some people and not to others? This book explores a multitude of factors on three levels: spiritual, psychological, and physical. Topics include agreements, life path, soul chemistry, male/female energy ratio, celibacy, body-type attraction, sexual orientation, monogamy, and polyfidelity.

REVIEWS

What an amazing book! Reading this was a pure joy.

I loved it! Brief and beautiful guidelines for "growing up" spiritually: being our own authority while also taking responsibility for the choices we make. I'm especially enjoying sitting with statements like this: "Peacefully holding the tension between our higher-self knowing and our lower-self conditioning can power the imprinting of our knowing into our lower self." Had never thought to put it that way, but it resonates deeply for me. Strongly recommend this unique take on true self-empowerment—and all in a quick read!

In succinct fashion, *All Is Choice* makes a strong case for why making conscious choices in word and action in all aspects of our lives leads to better outcomes for ourselves, family, friends, and the world.

A wonderful and easy read.

Loving it!

Printed in Great Britain
by Amazon